Zodiac Signs

DiscoverRoo
An Imprint of Pop!
popbooksonline.com

SCORPIO

by Elizabeth Andrews

WELCOME TO DiscoverRoo!

This book is filled with videos, puzzles, games, and more! Scan the QR codes* while you read, or visit the website below to make this book pop.

popbooksonline.com/scorpio

abdobooks.com
Published by Pop!, a division of ABDO, PO Box 398166, Minneapolis, Minnesota 55439.

Printed in the United States of America, North Mankato, Minnesota.

042025
082025

THIS BOOK CONTAINS RECYCLED MATERIALS

Cover Photo: Splendoura Prints; Shutterstock Images
Interior Photos: Getty Images; Shutterstock Images
Editor: Tyler Gieseke
Series Designer: Laura Graphenteen

Library of Congress Control Number: 2024948390

Publisher's Cataloging-in-Publication Data

Names: Andrews, Elizabeth, author.
Title: Scorpio / by Elizabeth Andrews
Description: Minneapolis, Minnesota : Pop!, 2026 | Series: Zodiac signs | Includes online resources and index
Identifiers: ISBN 9781098247959 (lib. bdg.) | ISBN 9781098248499 (ebook)
Subjects: LCSH: Scorpio (Astrology)--Juvenile literature. | Scorpion (Astrology)--Juvenile literature. | Scorpius (Astrology)--Juvenile literature. | Zodiac--Juvenile literature. | Astrology--Juvenile literature. | Astrology--Charts, diagrams, etc.--Juvenile literature.
Classification: DDC 133.52--dc23

*Scanning QR codes requires a web-enabled smart device with a QR code reader app and a camera.

TABLE OF CONTENTS

CHAPTER 1

MEET THE SCORPIO!

Scorpio is the eighth sign of the zodiac. People born between October 24 and November 21 are Scorpios. When people ask for your "star sign," they are likely asking for your sun sign. This is the zodiac sign the sun appeared in at your birth.

Geranium

WATCH A VIDEO HERE!

October 24–November 21

SCORPIO

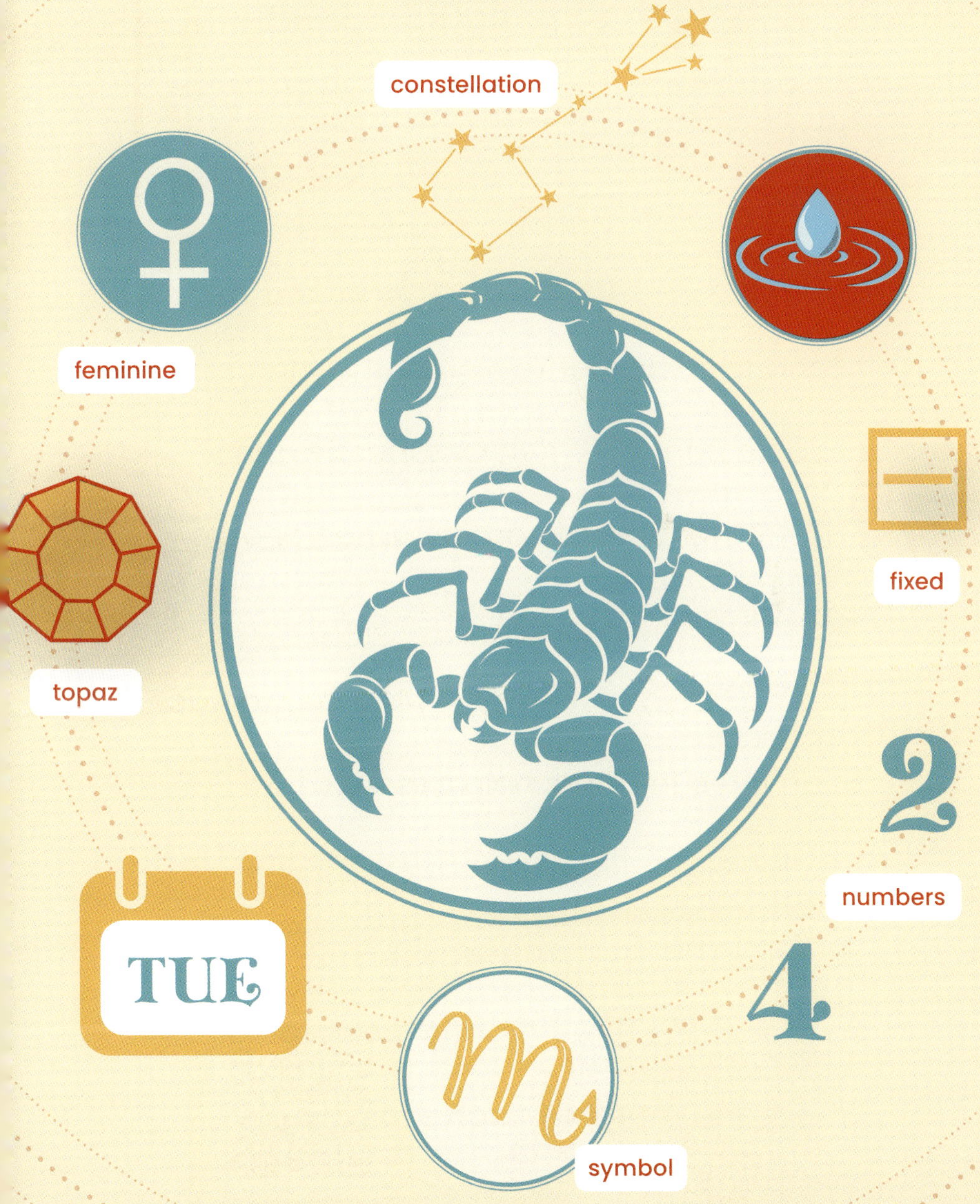

ZODIAC CALENDAR

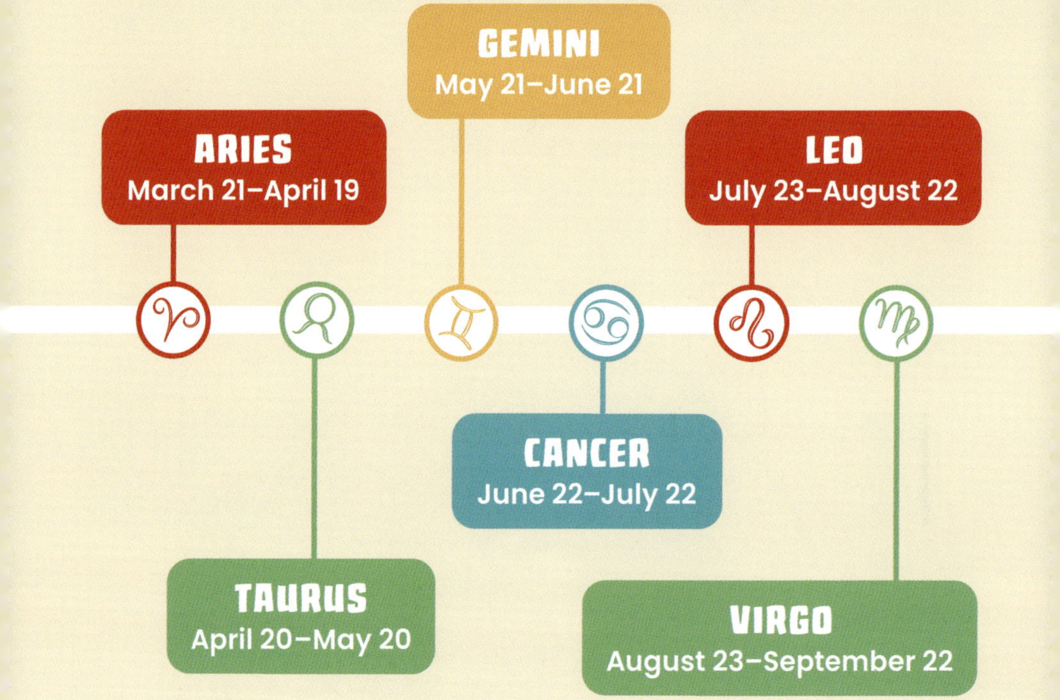

Three features help describe zodiac signs. Signs can be masculine or feminine. Each zodiac sign is given a mode. The three modes are cardinal, fixed, and mutable. Each zodiac is also

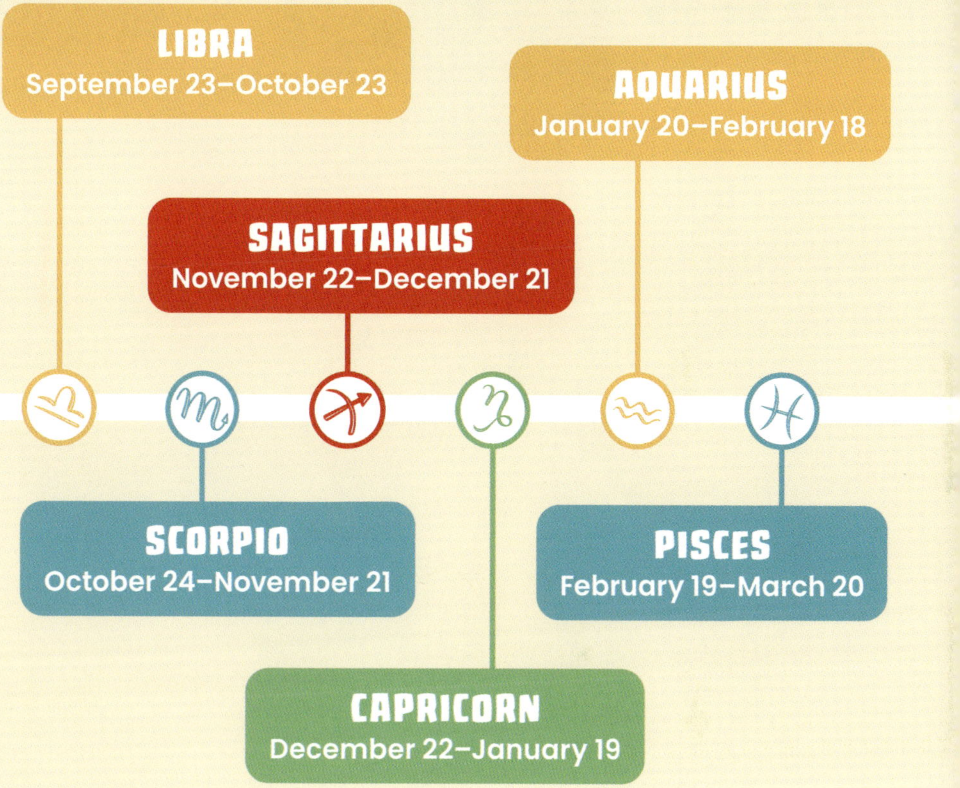

a fire, air, earth, or water sign. No zodiac sign shares the same three features.

DID YOU KNOW? Fixed signs are born in the middle of seasons. They can get stuck in their ways.

Feminine signs are usually present and calm.

Scorpio is a feminine, fixed, water sign. Feminine signs are grounded. Many of their actions are done **internally**. They are in touch with their own emotions and those around them.

Modes describe how signs interact with the outside world. Fixed signs are emotionally stable. They are clear thinkers. They don't like change. Water signs are emotional and observant. They are often **sentimental** and **sensitive**.

Water signs enjoy hearing stories of days gone by.

The constellation Orion is large and easy to find in the night sky.

Scorpio is **represented** by a scorpion. In ancient Greek mythology, the **constellation** Scorpius is the scorpion that killed the handsome hunter Orion. Orion said he could kill every animal on earth. This angered Artemis, the goddess of the hunt. She sent the scorpion to kill Orion. Ancient Babylonians also named the constellation after scorpions.

Scorpions are known for their painful and sometimes deadly sting.

CHAPTER 2

HISTORY OF ASTROLOGY

Humans have looked for life's **spiritual** meaning since the beginning of time. They often looked to the stars for this. Astrology is the practice of reading the movements of planets and other **celestial** bodies and connecting them to life on Earth.

LEARN MORE HERE!

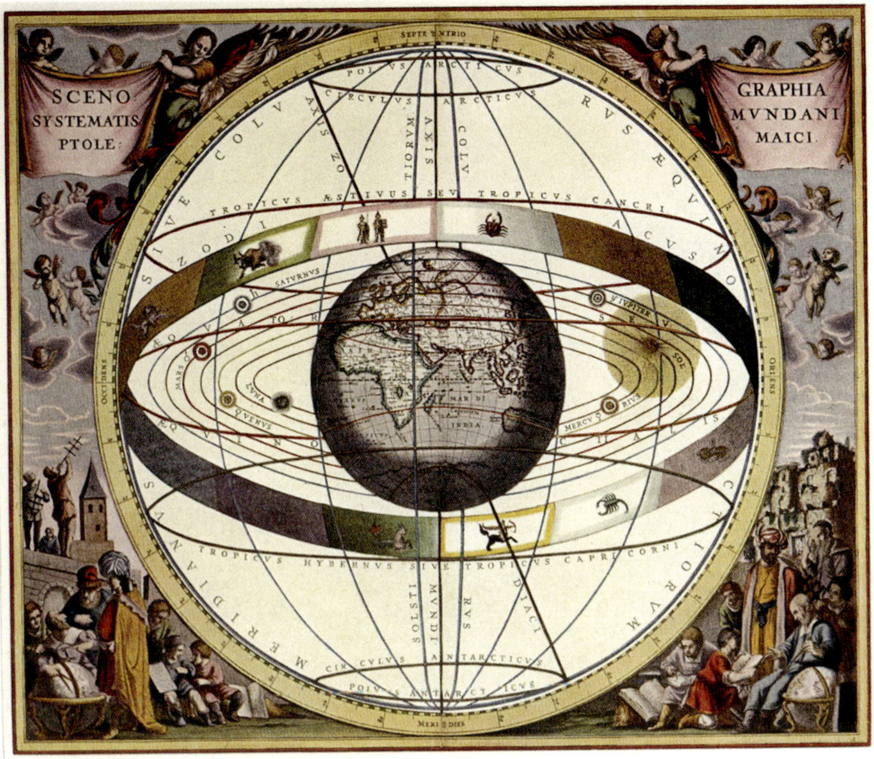

Some ancient people used the zodiac signs to predict future events.

Babylonians invented the zodiac in Mesopotamia over 5,000 years ago. Mesopotamia was the first known civilization. Babylon was one of the region's largest cities.

Ptolemy was an Egyptian man who studied the stars.

Earth and our solar system are in the Milky Way galaxy.

The zodiac is a belt of space around Earth that has 12 well-known **constellations**. Ancient people noticed that the sun seemed to move in front of these constellations throughout a year. The sun spends about a month in each constellation.

The constellations in the zodiac belt are Aries, Taurus, Gemini, Cancer, Leo, Virgo, Libra, Scorpius, Sagittarius, Capricornus, Aquarius, and Pisces. Together they make up the 12 zodiac signs. They are all **represented** by different **symbols**.

Islamic astrologers created new ways to map and measure stars.

THE ZODIAC WHEEL

DID YOU KNOW?

Most zodiac symbols are animals. The ancient Greeks called the belt of space *zodiakos kyklos,* or "circle of animals."

CHAPTER 3

FUELED BY FEELINGS

Scorpio is ruled by Pluto. Pluto is the planet of changes, mystery, and power. It was named after the Roman god of the underworld. The underworld is where souls go when they die in many ancient stories. Pluto is a fierce planet. It gives Scorpios strong emotions. Scorpios' connection to Pluto also helps them dive deep into life's mysteries.

Pluto had a three-headed guard dog named Cerberus.

EXPLORE LINKS HERE!

Scorpio is thought to be the most misunderstood sign. To most people, Scorpios are secretive and unapproachable. Scorpios do not like to show their emotions. They prefer to seem cool and calm. However, underneath

Claude Monet was a famous Scorpio painter. Some of his most well-known works feature water. Below is The Water Lily Pond *from 1899.*

Like a Scorpio, most of an iceberg's mass lies below the surface.

the surface, Scorpios have big feelings. These emotions are what drive Scorpios' choices and actions.

DID YOU KNOW?

Scorpios are like icebergs. Most of their feelings and personality are hidden.

Sometimes Scorpios ignore what they are really feeling. They try to fill their brain with other tasks.

The main thing all Scorpios want is control. If they are not working toward a goal, they will be unhappy. Some good ways for Scorpios to have control are by keeping their spaces clean, being of use to others, and bringing peace to unpleasant situations.

Most Scorpios believe they have a single great purpose. Scorpios try their best to find out what theirs is. Once they find their purpose, they work toward it with great focus. Scorpios will keep their plans to themselves until they have accomplished everything they wanted.

If a Scorpio's purpose is to be a baker, some goals might be to learn certain recipes.

CHAPTER 4

A SIGN WITH SMARTS

Scorpios are usually very smart, as are most water signs. Scorpios pay close attention to things happening around them. They are quick to understand new and interesting subjects. If something catches their attention, they want to know everything about it.

COMPLETE AN ACTIVITY HERE!

Topaz is the stone of strength and bravery.

Scorpios are good at learning new languages.

DID YOU KNOW?

Scorpios can sometimes sense things before they happen. All water signs tend to have this gift.

As doctors, Scorpios may try to learn how to fight specific diseases.

Scorpios make good doctors, scientists, and **spiritual** leaders. They prefer jobs that let them dive into things they care about. Scorpios also like helping people. Spiritual leaders help guide people to their best selves and make sense of life's mysteries. They often understand what is needed to lead people through difficult things.

Relationships can be hard for Scorpios. They keep many of their feelings hidden. But they also pay close attention to people around them. Often, Scorpios show the best and worst of themselves to the people closest to them. They are generous and loving to friends, family, and partners. They can also be distrustful and show darker moods.

Everything a Scorpio does or feels is intense.

Scorpius is best viewed in July.

Loyalty is important to Scorpios. They are always willing to help. They get very **attached** to people, places, and things that they care about. Scorpios are competitive. They will also hold onto anger and plan to get back at someone if they feel they have been wronged. This is their scorpion sting.

Today, astrology can answer questions about an individual. People use astrology to understand who they are and why they might do what they do. It can also help them understand other people in their life. A zodiac sign can point out personal skills, possibilities, and **internal motivations**.

WHAT IS A BIRTH CHART?

Each person's birth chart contains all the planets in our solar system, the moon, and the sun. The location of where each **celestial** body was based on the exact time and location of a person's birth can be marked on a birth chart. A birth chart can explain even more about a person than what only a sun sign can. The placement of each planet affects the drive of a person. This reveals personal motivations. Astrology experts can read birth charts.

MAKING CONNECTIONS

TEXT-TO-SELF

Are you a Scorpio? If so, do you think the sign matches your personality? If not, what do you have in common with Scorpio?

TEXT-TO-TEXT

Have you read any books about the other zodiac signs? How were those signs similar to and different from Scorpio?

TEXT-TO-WORLD

With the help of an adult, look up famous Scorpios. Pick one person and write a few sentences about ways that person shows Scorpio qualities.

GLOSSARY

attached — feeling strong affection for and not wanting to part with.

celestial — having to do with the sky or outer space.

constellation — a group of stars that forms a pattern.

internal — of, relating to, or being on the inside.

motivation — something that makes one want to do something.

represent — to stand for or be a sign of.

sensitive — feeling or noticing things quite sharply.

sentimental — causing or showing tender feelings.

spiritual — having to do with people's beliefs in things such as the soul, nature, and what happens after death.

symbol — an object or picture that represents something else.

INDEX

DiscoverRoo!

ONLINE RESOURCES

This book is filled with videos, puzzles, games, and more! Scan the QR codes* while you read, or visit the website below to make this book pop.

popbooksonline.com/scorpio

*Scanning QR codes requires a web-enabled smart device with a QR code reader app and a camera.